First published in 2003 by Watling St Publishing
The Glen
Southrop
Lechlade
Gloucestershire
GL7 3NY

Printed in Italy

ISBN 1-904153-13-5

24681097531

Design: Maya Currell
Cover design and illustration: Mark Davis
Cartoons: Martin Angel

# Highwaymen, Outlaws and Bandits of London

# Highwaymen, Outlaws and Bandits of London

### Travis Elborough

WATLING STREET

Travis Elborough is a freelance writer who lives in North London. Once upon a time he hoped to buy a sprawling Bavarian castle and spend the dark hours building a hideous monster in a custom-built laboratory housed in the basement. But these days he can't help thinking that the whole mad scientist thing has become such a cliché and would happily settle for a garden flat with period features in NW5.

This book is for Lauren.

# Contents

# INTRODUCTION

Today when we think of outlaws and bandits we tend to think of the American Wild West – wagon trains and cowboys and Indians – but for centuries London was plagued by masked raiders. It was the Wild West End. Travellers were constantly at risk from being robbed by highwaymen (and women) who stalked the roads in and out of the city. Swanky areas like Knightsbridge, Kensington, Putney and Clapham – which were then just leafy villages on the edge of town – were hotspots for highwaymen. It wasn't safe to stray onto Hampstead Heath, Finchley Common or even Hyde Park at night.

As we'll discover, it wasn't much safer slap in the centre of town either. Highwaymen and pickpockets prowled in

Piccadilly and even right outside the Houses of Parliament! Until the 1800s the theft of anything worth more than a shilling (12 old pence) was punishable by death. So most highwaymen ended up swinging from the gallows at Tyburn, now Marble Arch.

In this book we'll meet London's nastiest and nicest outlaws. We'll meet chivalrous 'gentlemen of the road', trendy thieves and the capital's most callous conwoman! We'll meet ugly thugs, friendly fops and a rapping robber.

Before we get to hear the clatter of hooves and the cry of 'Stand and deliver' from highwaymen such as Dick Turpin, we need to go back a little further in time to meet England's most famous outlaw.

# CHAPTER ONE

# Robin the Robber

This is difficult for a Londoner to admit but (grit teeth) England's oldest bandit – Robin Hood – probably never set foot in the capital. Before you get too excited, Robin did have a good excuse for not popping by. He may never have existed at all …

Stories about Robin of Sherwood Forest and his band of merry men are as old as the hills (maybe even older). The tales are so old that we have no idea if they are true or not, or even who Robin Hood might have been. For all we know, the real Robin could have been a vicious bandit who mercilessly plundered anyone foolish enough to stray into the forest.

In ancient times, particularly on long winter evenings, people would gather by the fireside and tell each other stories. There were no televisions or newspapers and very few books. These really were the dark ages! Good storytellers were always in demand. No one cared if they made things up or exaggerated as long as they told smashing stories. A good story usually needs a hero, a villain and a heroine just as it needs a beginning, a middle and an end.

Just think if, on some dark and stormy night, you had to listen to this ...

*Once upon a time there was a nasty horrible crook called Robin Hood. Robin lived in Sherwood Forest and stole things from anyone who crossed his path. The end.*

... it'd be a bit boring, wouldn't it? And Robin doesn't sound too nice either.

You'd want something more exciting. What's up with this Robin guy anyway? Why is he living in a forest? Why is he stealing things? What's his motivation? Is he poor? Or, is he just plain greedy?

A storyteller could help by explaining how and why Robin became a bandit. To make Robin more likeable they might gloss over some of his bad points. Before long Robin the

Rotten Crook became Robin the Brave Yeoman forced into exile. Add an evil villain – the Sheriff of Nottingham – and a beautiful damsel in distress – Maid Marion – and we are really talking! Will the good guy get the girl? Or will the bad old sheriff triumph? Bung in an archery contest and some cool green costumes and you've got a hit!

Imagine if you were a poor farmer or blacksmith in those days. Tales about an outlaw who righted wrongs and stole from the rich and gave to the poor really would be thrilling! In an age when the poor were treated like animals, Robin is the champion of the underdog. Robin might be a thief but he stood for justice and equality.

Robin wasn't only popular with ordinary people. The young King Henry VIII – the serial husband from hell – was a huge fan of Robin Hood. In 1510 Henry held a Robin Hood-style archery contest at Shooter's Hill near Blackheath. The king and his men dressed in suits

of green and pretended to be outlaws to entertain his young queen, Catherine of Aragon. (She was lucky – later horrible Henry stopped entertaining his wives and started executing them!)

Robin may be a myth but in the Middle Ages robbers and bandits did hide in the woods and forests. Like Robin they loved stealing from the rich. Unfortunately, they weren't so keen on giving to the poor!

By horrible Henry's time the woodland robber was out of date. Towns and cities were in. More and more people were living in them. Outlaws could hang about in the woods all day long but if no one passed by they had no one to rob.

What was the biggest city in Tudor England? London. In 1500 about 40,000 people lived in the capital. London was five times bigger than the next biggest city, Norwich. The crooks were coming to town!

Tudor London was a thief's dream. There was no proper police force. It was stuffed with rich people practically begging to be robbed. A pickpocket could make off with a purse and then slip quietly away in the crowds. The roads in and out of the city were always packed with wealthy travellers – easy meat for hungry thieves.

In 1497 one Italian visitor to England noted that 'few venture to go alone in the country, excepting in the middle of the day, and few still in the towns at night, and least of all in London.'

Most robbers who 'worked' in and around London were little different from modern muggers. They robbed on foot and so were called 'footpads'. They either grabbed what they wanted or threatened people with knives until they handed over their loot. Hardly glamorous, is it?

Not all crooks fancied life as a footpad. There was a lot of legwork for a start! It was risky and exhausting. London's streets didn't help. They were muddy tracks with big smelly drains full of poo running slap down the middle of them! Think if you slipped while running away ...

A robber on a horse, now ... they could make a quick getaway. The robber could concentrate on the threatening talking and let the horse do the walking. Riding a horse is not as easy as it looks. As with car drivers, some people are much better at it than others. In the centuries before flash cars, to own a good horse was a sign of wealth. Kings, like horrible Henry, prided themselves on their horseriding skills. (Today, horse racing is still called the sport of kings.) A thief who rode a horse believed he or she was a better class of crook.

Highwaymen (and women) were much more mobile than other thieves. They could rob several coaches across the city on the same day and still ride off to a secret hideout. Dashing about on a great big horse was more exciting than running about on foot. A horse-riding highwayman (or woman) had to be bold and brave. Storytellers began to talk about their exploits. They borrowed from the Robin Hood legends and glossed over the bad bits. Soon stories about handsome highwaymen were the latest craze. Some highwaymen were flattered and even tried to live up to their reputation!

Even the great playwright William Shakespeare – who lived in Southwark when Elizabeth I was queen – got in on the act. In his historical play *Henry IV* the future king of

England, Prince Hal, is involved in robbing a group of travellers at Gad's Hill in Kent. (Can you see Prince Charles or Prince William as highway robbers?) Gad's Hill was the main road from Kent to London and a prime spot for highwaymen. Shakespeare makes Hal a highwayman to show that he will become a brave fighting king.

In the next chapter we'll meet some more posh highwaymen who robbed for a taste of adventure.

# CHAPTER TWO

# Noble Rogues

## The Wrong Arm of the Law: The Highwayman Who Became a Judge

Johnny Popham was a bright spark. He did well at school and went to Oxford – one of England's best universities – in the 1550s. His teachers thought he would go far. Young Johnny had other ideas. He was fed up with stuffy books. What was the point in becoming a doctor or a lawyer if it meant spending even more time reading dull books.

(Obviously Johnny died years before Harry Potter, Lemony Snicket and the wonderful *Ghosts, Ghouls and Phantoms of London* published by Watling Street and available now in all good bookshops and some of the bad ones too!)

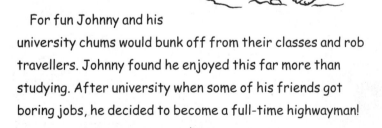

For fun Johnny and his university chums would bunk off from their classes and rob travellers. Johnny found he enjoyed this far more than studying. After university when some of his friends got boring jobs, he decided to become a full-time highwayman!

# WANTED: HIGHWAYMAN

## Dealing in Stealing
## Tobygloak Temps Ltd

Are you looking for excitement?

Love horses and the open road?

Know how to point a pistol?

Do you fancy wearing a neat mask?

## Have you ever considered becoming a highwayman?

If you are a lone crook or a team player, highway robbery could

be just the job for you!

## Our Highwaymen enjoy:

- Flexible working hours
- Great performance-related pay scheme — the more you rob the more money you make!
- A chance to meet the rich and famous — and steal from them!

**Apply in person to**
**Tobygloak Temps Ltd**
**The Spaniard's Inn**
**Hampstead**
**London**

Tobygloak Temps Ltd values a devious workforce.
Applications from retired pickpockets and disgruntled
royalists particularly welcome.

**(Applicants must have their own horse and pistols)**

Johnny spent the next ten years robbing on the roads. He was happy as a highwayman. His wife wasn't. When Mrs Popham had first met Johnny, they had both been very young. Having a boyfriend who was a highwayman had been thrilling. All her friends had been jealous. Johnny looked so handsome on a horse. But now, all her friends had settled down. Their husbands had proper jobs. They lived in nice houses. Their husbands came home for tea each evening. Johnny was out robbing as soon as it got dark. Their husbands wore nice clothes to work. Johnny wore a cloak and a mask. (Mrs P hated washing them. She couldn't hang them on the line to dry in case someone saw them!)

Sometimes Johnny disappeared for days on end and Mrs P was left to worry herself sick about him. Had he been shot in a robbery? Had he been caught? Would he be hanged?

She decided enough was enough. When Johnny came home one evening she sat him down, gave him a glass of wine and told him it was high time he gave up highway robbery.

'Look Johnny,' she said, 'lawyers make pots of money. You could make more keeping the law rather than breaking it. If you went on to become a judge you could still dress up in a big robe. You'd even get to wear a wig instead of that grubby old mask of yours.'

Judges began wearing wigs in medieval times.
Bald monks used to cover their heads with a piece
of white cloth when they were acting as judges.
For some reason the look took off and judges
have worn wigs ever since!

Johnny liked the sound of a wig and gown. He hung up his mask and cloak and went back to study law.

Johnny did well this time round. He passed his exams with flying colours and got a job working in the Middle Temple – the heart of London's legal profession. He later became a member of Parliament and received a knighthood. In 1581 he was made Lord Chief Justice – the top job for an English judge. He was responsible for the trials of the explorer Sir Walter Raleigh and Gunpowder Plotter Guy Fawkes!

You might think that a former crook would be kind to other criminals. Not Johnny, he was a tough judge. He once sentenced a member of his old highway gang to death!

After passing the death sentence Johnny asked the man what had happened to the rest of the gang. The man replied: 'All the villains are hanged, my lord, except you and me.' So that meant only Johnny was left after the trial!

## The Rhyming Robber

John Clavell was from a posh family. His uncle, Sir William Clavell, was loaded and a good mate of King Charles I. John's relatives may have had money but John was always stony broke. Like Johnny Popham he was good at school but at university he got into debt.  He borrowed money from a loan shark (someone who lends money but charges you a fortune to repay it). John found he couldn't afford to pay his loan back and so started stealing.

Yet another relatively useless bit of information...

Queen Elizabeth I was a huge fan of bear-baiting and regularly watched contests at Southwark.

To make matters worse, John had also become addicted to gambling. John bet on cards, the toss of a coin and bear-baiting contests. Wild bears were once common in England and were used for entertainment. Large crowds used to gather to watch bears fight dogs in contests. It was once London's most popular sport.

If there were no cards, coins or bears about he'd happily bet on the weather or even the weight of a piece of cheese. John just loved to gamble. Unfortunately, he was never very lucky. If he said heads it was tails. In cards, if John said twist, he went bust. If he insisted it would be sunny, it rained. As for the weight of a piece of cheese ... well ... enough said.

To pay off his huge debts John hooked up with a soldier friend – who was also short of cash – and became a highwayman. Together they robbed mail coaches on the roads into London and at Gad's Hill in Kent.

John was his own worst enemy. Sometimes he'd gamble away the booty even before the robbery had taken place …

'John, I bet you that this coach coming along here will be loaded with loot!'

'Okay, I bet you that it isn't.'

'How much do want to bet on that?'

'Well, if you're right you get to you keep the loot. If I am right, I get to keep it.'

'Done!' ('You have been,' his partner sniggered under his breath.)

John and his partner were caught and arrested during a robbery at Shooter's Hill near Blackheath in 1627. John was locked up in the King's Bench Prison in Southwark. While he was in gaol he gave up gambling and took up writing poetry. He decided to write a poem to his uncle's friend King Charlie begging to be pardoned. The robber became a rapper!

Here's his poem to Charlie.

> I that have robbed so oft am now bid stand,
> Death and the Law assault me demand
> My Life and means, I never used me go
> But having taken their money let them go
> Yet must I die? And, is there no relief?
> The King of Kings had mercy on a thief!

It may not be very good but it worked. King Charlie let John off!

John followed the poem with his autobiography. He called it *A Recantation of an Ill-Led Life*. It became a bestseller. John then went on to write a play, *The Soddered Citizen*. It was a hit comedy and William Shakespeare's old theatre company, The King's Men, performed it at the Globe Theatre! Pleased with his successes John gave up writing. He moved to Ireland and is thought to have worked as a lawyer until his death in 1642.

# Chapter Three

# How To Be a Highwayman

Francis Jackson was another robber who was a writer. Frank wasn't as lucky as our rapping robber, John Clavell. On 16 March 1674, Frank and his gang had been robbing near Hounslow and were making their way home. All of a sudden they were set upon by an angry mob of local people armed with clubs. The locals, fed up with these nasty highwaymen, wanted to teach Frank and co a lesson they wouldn't forget. (They planned to go nightclubbing! Groan.) Frank and his friends managed to fight them off. They escaped but the locals gave chase. They raced through Paddington and Kilburn but the mob were hot on their tail. The mob finally caught up with the highwaymen at Hampstead and handed them over to the authorities. Frank was sentenced to death and hanged at Tyburn on 15 April 1674.

Just before he was executed Frank wrote all about his life as a highwayman. His book was published after his death. It had a very long and very odd title. It was called:

*Jackson's Recantation, or the Life and Death of the Notorious Highwayman now hanging in chains at Hampstead. Delivered to a Friend a little before Execution; wherein is truly discovered the whole Mystery of that Wicked and*

*Fatal Profession of Padding on the Road.*

Snappy, eh?

# Highwayman Hotspot

The bodies of the most notorious highwaymen were put on display to serve as a warning to others. Poor Frank Jackson suffered this fate.

After being hanged Frank's body was thrown into a cauldron of boiling pitch – a foul sticky black mixture normally used on roofs. Once Frank's body was completely coated in pitch it was fished out and wrapped in chains. This wasn't to stop Frank running away again (it was too late for that!), the chains were used to secure the body to a post. The post was called a 'gibbet'.

Look, I'm late for my 5 o'clock meeting

Frank was gibbeted at North End, Hampstead, but there were gibbets all over London. They were usually placed on the main roads into the city – the same roads plagued by robbers and highwaymen. (Some deterrent!) As well as Hampstead in North London there were gibbets at Highgate and Finchley.

25

In the south, Wimbledon and Putney had gibbets. There were even gibbets in swanky Kensington and Knightsbridge, which were then just villages on the edge of the city. Today visitors to London meet signs welcoming them to the city. In days gone by travellers were greeted by rotting bodies, swinging in chains. This grim practice wasn't abolished until 1834.

Frank's book was full of secrets about highway robbery. Travellers loved it. It had great tips on how to avoid being robbed. It became the essential guidebook for visitors to London! Would-be highwaymen loved it too. It had great tips on how to rob on the road. It also became the essential training manual for highwaymen. It was a huge success.

## Frank's Top Tips For Highwaymen

*A horse – make sure it's well fed and watered, a hungry horse doesn't run as fast as a full one.*

*A good old-fashioned three-cornered hat – the essential hat for highwaymen. The jauntier the better. When robbing you can pull it down low to cover your face!*

*A pocket handkerchief – they make very handy masks. Just make sure it doesn't have a name tag or initials sewn on it!*

Lots of wigs and fake beards – you never know when you'll need a new disguise!

A pebble – put it in your mouth to hide the sound of your own voice!

Secret code words – if anyone overhears you they won't suspect that you plan to rob them!

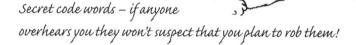

Sunday is a great day for robbing. The roads into London are quieter so it's easier to escape!

## Frank's Top Tips For Travellers

Money – take as little with you as possible and never tell anyone how much cash you have on you.

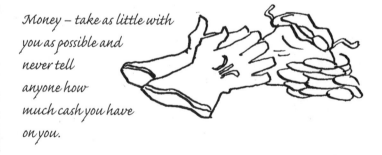

Good old-fashioned three-cornered hats – be suspicious of anyone wearing one. Highwaymen love good old-fashioned three-cornered hats. They think they look jaunty.

*Strange-coloured hair or beards – be suspicious of anyone with an odd-coloured beard or hair. Highwaymen often wear wigs or beards to disguise themselves.*

*Sunday – avoid travelling on Sundays. The roads into London are quieter and easier for highwaymen to get away.*

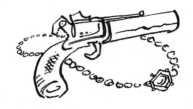

# CHAPTER FOUR

# Royalist Robbers

King Charles I was the highwaymen's favourite sort of king. He was a dandy, a seventeenth-century fashion victim. He wore jaunty hats, frilly shirts and had a snazzy goatee beard. (He also had a lisp. Highwaymen who used Frank Jackson's tip about putting a pebble in their mouths sounded just like Charlie!) He loved playing bowls, riding horses and collecting jewels and paintings. So did all his friends and he held grand banquets at his palace in Whitehall. On such days the roads would be packed with rich peers making their way to and from the capital. Easy game for highwaymen.

Unfortunately not everyone approved of the king and his lavish lifestyle. Fashions were changing. The Puritans, a religious movement, believed that simple things were better. Frilly shirts were out. They preferred plain clothes, short, pudding-bowl haircuts and thought that having too much cash was a bad thing. It was all very well for Charlie and his mates to swan around Covent Garden in jaunty hats and snazzy goatee beards but someone had to pay for it. The government, led by the Puritan Oliver Cromwell, was getting fed up with forking out for Charlie's paintings and parties. The row between Charlie and Oliver spiralled into a full-blown civil war. The country was divided between Royalists or Cavaliers who remained loyal to the king (in frilly shirts, sporting natty beards) and Oliver's pudding-bowl-haired Roundheads or Parliamentarians.

Most highwaymen sided with the king, perhaps you can guess why...

Picture the scene ... Hampstead Heath about 7 o'clock on a chilly November evening in 1643. A coach is weaving its way across the heath when two masked men on horseback suddenly appear ...

'Stand and deliver! Your money or your life! Come on! We haven't got all night. Hand over your jewels, watches and trinkets!'

'I am terribly sorry, Mr Highwayman, but we are simple Puritans. We have no frivolous jewels or trinkets.'

'What? Well, just give me your money.'

'Again, sir, we don't believe in worldly goods. Here, take my purse, I think it has a few pence in it.'

The highwayman grabs the purse and peers inside.

'Four pence! Is that all you've got? That wouldn't even keep my horse in oats. What use is four pence to me? I don't know what this country is coming to. You lot are ruining things. How's a highwaymen

supposed to make an honest living? Give me Charlie and his gang any day, at least they have the decency to travel around loaded with loot. Come on, Jake, let's head off to Finchley – we might catch the last mail coach if we're lucky.'

Some highwaymen even joined the Royalist forces and fought as cavalrymen. The English Civil War lasted for six years but finally Oliver Cromwell's Parliamentarians were victorious. On 30 January 1649 Charles I was beheaded outside his own Banqueting Hall at Whitehall. With the war over many old highwaymen went back to robbing on the roads. They were joined by Royalist officers on the run from Oliver's army. These Knights of the Road were trained soldiers who prided themselves on their bravery and their good manners. They may have been desperate outlaws armed with pistols but they tried to remember their 'please's and thank you's' too.

## The Courteous Captain

Captain James Hind was just such an outlaw. James, like the notorious highwayman Dick Turpin (more about him later), trained as a butcher. It wasn't long however before he grew to hate the smell of pork chops. He was sick of getting his clothes covered in blood and thoroughly fed up with sharpening knives and washing chopping boards. It was dull. He wanted some fresh air and adventure.

One evening he met Thomas Allen, a highwayman, in a pub on Fleet Street. The pair got chatting and Tom asked James to join his highway gang. A few nights later James was holding up coaches on Shooters Hill in Woolwich and enjoying every minute of it. He got to gallop across the city, wear a great mask, the hours were good and the money ... well, he'd have to have hacked up every pig in Smithfield's meat market to make as much. Curiously, though, while James loved the cash and cutting a dash on his horse, he found he felt rather sorry for his victims. For this reason he always tried to be as nice as possible. Sometimes, so as not to appear greedy, he would let travellers hang on to a few guineas (gold pieces) or keep their favourite watches or rings. Stories about the exploits of this courteous highwayman began to spread. Other highwaymen, worried that they might be missing out on a whole new robbing racket, copied him. London's highwaymen soon gained a reputation as the politest in the whole of Europe.

When the Civil War broke out James was twenty-six years old and, keen to do his bit for king and country, he joined the Royalist army. He was made a captain and even fought bravely alongside the king's son, Charles (later King Charles II), at the disastrous Battle of Worcester. The King's forces were thrashed and James had to sneak back to London. He hid in a room above a barber's shop near St Dunstan's Church on Fleet Street. So that no one would recognize him, he wore a wig and adopted a false name, James Brown. (I wonder how long that took him to think up.) Following Charles's execution he decided to wage his own one-man war against the Puritans. From now on he would only rob Puritan coaches and he did, politely refusing to take money from anyone who would swear undying loyalty to the Crown. On one occasion he succeeded in holding up the Roundhead leader, Oliver Cromwell himself. Unluckily, Oliver's carriage was guarded by heavily armed soldiers and James had to bid a hasty retreat. By now there was a price on his head. A nasty neighbour keen to get his grubby mitts on the reward betrayed James to Oliver's men and he was arrested and hauled off to Newgate Prison.

## Nauseous Newgate

Newgate Prison was London's most notorious and most disgusting prison. For nearly eight hundred years it stood where The Old Bailey — our largest law courts — are today in the City (the home of London's biggest businesses). From its earliest days it was famed for being a stinking, horrible hole. Most of London's highwaymen were imprisoned there.

Oliver was worried that James's mates might stir up trouble in London. He sent James to Worcester and had him hanged there without a fuss on 24 September 1652.

# Highwayman Hotspot

Abiezer Coppe was not a highwayman but a Puritan preacher. He was a completely manic, street preacher. He believed that the world was going to end and often visited London to spread his gloomy message. He would tour the city bellowing at anyone who would listen. Passers-by, coach drivers, women with babies, dogs and statues were told to change their ways or face a horrible, usually fiery, death.

In 1650 he wrote a very odd little book, *A Fiery Flying Roll*, where he announced that God would return to earth as a highwayman. According to Abiezer, God would ride around England taking money from the greedy and giving it to the needy. The government, worried that this would encourage ordinary highwaymen, flung Abiezer in Newgate Gaol. They confiscated all the copies of *A Fiery Flying Roll* they could find and publicly burnt them at the New Palace Yard, Westminster, and at the market places in Cheapside and Southwark. (What a scorcher!)

### Another relatively useless bit of information ...

In the newspapers of the time Abiezer was nicknamed 'The Ranter', after the Dutch word 'ranten' which means to rave or shout like a mad thing. We still use the word 'rant' today.

# Mulled Sack, the Boozy Bandit

Even in London during the 1600s Mulled was not a common first name. Thomas, Mary, Sarah were popular. There was the odd Ebenezer and Elsbeth. Royalists were keen on Charles for boys. Puritans favoured Oliver. But Mulled? Surely no one called their sons or their daughters that? Well, our next Royalist robber really was known as Mulled Sack. His parents actually gave him the far more sensible name of John Cottingham. However, John was just so fond of mulled sack, a spicy wine drink that was a bit like a seventeenth-century cola, that everyone called him Mulled. (Everyone except his mum, that is, she simply hated the nickname.)

Born in Cheapside, London, in 1614 Mulled was working as a chimney sweep by the time he was eight years old. (Until the late 1800s children were forced to earn a living cleaning out sooty chimneys. Charles Dickens, the great London novelist

wrote all about it in his book *Oliver Twist*.) At thirteen
Mulled fell in with a rough crowd. He abandoned his sweep's
brushes and took up pickpocketing. Mulled was extremely
nimble-fingered and soon had stolen enough loot to 'have
built St Paul's cathedral', it was said.

Mulled was a bit of a snob. He was embarrassed about
being a pickpocket. Pickpockets were the lowest of the
low. They were sneaky, devious types. Even pickpockets
hated pickpockets. Highway robbery – now that was a
proper crime. None of this fishing about in strangers'
pockets. Mulled bought himself a horse and before long
he was a fully-fledged Knight of the Road. His favourite
patch was Hounslow Heath. After a good night's robbing on
the Heath he'd ride back across London to spend his booty
on (yes, you've guessed it) mulled sack in the Devil's Tavern
in the City.

Like Captain James Hind, Mulled was a big fan of King
Charlie (No 1), and he too was very particular about whom he
robbed. He only ever stole from Roundheads. In his most
daring robbery he held up a Roundhead army wagon on the
road from London to Oxford (now the A10). The wagon was
carrying wages for Oliver's soldiers. With the help of some
friends, Mulled made off with over £4000, an absolute
fortune then. Oliver and his soldiers, who'd had their hard-
earned pay nicked, were furious. A hunt for Mulled was

launched. He was finally caught near Reading and taken back to London and imprisoned in Newgate Prison. It was there that poor Mulled had his very last glass of sack. In the spring of 1659 he was sentenced to death and hanged at Smithfields.

# CHAPTER FIVE

# Dandy Highwaymen

In 1660 Oliver Cromwell died. Parliament decided it missed having a king about the place. They asked Charlie's son, Charles, if he would like to be king. Charles accepted. He had been living in France where he had gained a taste for the finer things in life. He loved good wine, tasty food and trendy clothes. Like his dad, he was a bit of a dandy. Following eleven years of stuffy Puritan rule England was rather pleased to have a glamorous king again. Frilly shirts were back in, much to the delight of highwaymen, old and new. Huzzah!

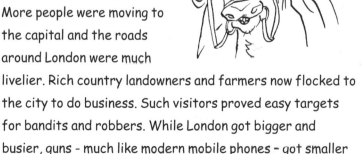

The city of London was also changing. After the Great Fire of London in 1666, new houses had been built and the city was growing in size. More people were moving to the capital and the roads around London were much livelier. Rich country landowners and farmers now flocked to the city to do business. Such visitors proved easy targets for bandits and robbers. While London got bigger and busier, guns - much like modern mobile phones – got smaller and more reliable. These new dinky pistols were perfect for highwaymen. They could still only fire a single shot but they were easier to load and carry while riding a horse. The true golden age of the highwayman had begun.

## The Elegant Iceman

In the winter of 1683 London was hit by a bitterly cold frost. It was so icy that the river Thames froze over for thirteen weeks! There was so much ice on the roads that it was impossible to get in and out of the city. Londoners decided to stay put and simply enjoy themselves. Great 'Frost Fairs', carnivals with stalls and competitions, were held on top of the frozen river. The well-to-do went ice-skating and the Thames quickly became the place to be seen. John Evelyn – a London diarist like the more famous Samuel Pepys – recorded watching sledge races and puppet shows on the ice.

While this was all great fun it was a complete disaster for highwaymen. With the roads icy and empty they had no way of making any cash. (Their assets were frozen!) Some got so desperate that they resorted to pickpocketing, mugging or burglary but one highwayman, Jonathan Simpson, had a better idea. He sold his horse and bought a pair of ice skates. He would dress in his best clothes and elegantly skate alongside the posh folk. When Jonathan spotted a rich skater on their own he'd follow them and chat about the weather or the result of the latest sledge race. When the moment was right, he'd trip them up and demand their money at gunpoint. Most handed their gold and jewels over without a murmur. By the time they had struggled to their feet to raise the alarm, Jonathan had skated clean away.

As the weather slowly improved cracks began to appear in the ice (and in Jonathan's scam). One fateful day, as Jonathan started to make his getaway, his right skate clipped a crack and he fell over. His victim pounced on him and Jonathan was swiftly bundled off to gaol. He was found guilty of robbery but mysteriously was let off at the very last minute. The Iceman melted away!

# The Thief of Hearts

Claude Duvall was once England's most famous highwayman –
which was quite an achievement because Claude was French.
Claude came to London in 1660 to work as a footman to the
Duke of Richmond. Claude liked his job. He had a neat
uniform and he rather enjoyed hanging about near the
Duke and his posh mates. However, as much as he warmed
to London he found that he still missed France. He became
so homesick that the thought of a jaunty little French dog
was enough to bring a tear to his eye. He began to neglect
his job and he was sacked.

He toyed with going home but he was so broke he
couldn't afford the boat across the channel. He could have
tried to get another job but he'd had enough of serving
ungrateful English gentleman. He decided instead to become
a highwayman. But not just any old highwaymen, though.
Oh no, Claude decided that he would become the greatest
'Gentleman of the Road' England had ever seen. Dressed
in his snappy French threads he would be Duvall the Dandy,
Duvall the Daring, Duvall the Dashing and Duvall the
Debonair. (He was keen on words beginning with the
letter D.)

Claude speedily made his name as a handsome highwayman.
Within weeks of taking to the road the pages of the *London
Gazette* newspaper were stuffed with stories about this

gallant Gallic gent. Everyone was talking about his exploits.
He was a seventeenth-century 'babe magnet', the Pop Idol of
his day. The Cockney poet Leigh Hunt said that Duvall was
'an eternal feather in the cap of gentility'. In other words,
Claude really was the bee's knees. He was so charming that
young girls dreamed of being robbed by him. Boys copied the
way he dressed and spoke. His favourite haunt was along
what is today the Bayswater Road. Coach parties would drive
along it in the hope of spotting him at work or, even better,
being held up themselves.

During one hold-up on Hampstead Heath, a wealthy
woman in the coach played a tune for him on a little wooden
flute. Claude was so flattered that he whipped out his own
flute and they played a duet! The pair then danced across
the Heath.

A couple of years later, the authorities finally captured Claude in the Hole-in-the-Wall Tavern on Chandos Street, near the Strand. The dandiest highwayman of all time was too drunk to escape! He was so smashed he had to be carried all the way to Newgate Prison! When he'd sobered up he was sentenced to death.

On the morning of Friday 21 January 1670, he was taken in a cart to Tyburn (where Marble Arch is now) to be hanged. Crying women lined the route and showered him in flowers. As he mounted the scaffold Claude turned to face the crowd. He was frightened but determined to go out in style. He pretended that this wasn't really his execution but the grand finale to his long and glittering career. He imagined that he was being presented with a big 'You're the Greatest Highwayman Ever' award. He'd even prepared a special speech to say thank you to his friends and admirers. The nasty hangman, Jack Ketch, however, ruined his plans. Before he could get the speech out of his pocket Jack had slung the noose over his head and kicked the ladder away.

His body was taken to the Tangier Tavern in St Giles near Covent Garden where it lay in state. Hundreds of men and women visited the tavern and placed bouquets at his feet and drank to his memory. (Not much comfort to Claude!) He was then buried in St Paul's church in Covent Garden. A poem celebrating his mischievous life was carved onto his tombstone. The stone was destroyed years ago but the poem has survived:

Here lies Duvall: Reader, if Male thou art,
Look to thy purse; if Female to thy heart
Old Tyburn's Glory, England's illustrious thief,
Duvall, the Ladies' Joy; Duvall, the Ladies' Grief.

# The Dynamic Duo: Maclean and Plunkett

In his day James Maclean was known as 'The Gentleman Highwayman'. He may have been a gent but he was as bent as they came. James was born in Monaghan, Ireland in 1724. His dad, Lauchlin, was a vicar. Lauchlin was a loving father but strict and a wee bit stingy. He never spent a penny, let alone a pound, if he could help it. Lauchlin firmly believed that if you looked after the pennies, the pounds looked much bigger. Especially when you could stack them up in great piles on the kitchen table (something Lauchlin enjoyed doing on damp winter evenings). Lauchlin wasn't a bad dad. He only saved his money so that his children could have a good education. (In those days there were no state schools and if you wanted an education you had to pay for it.) James's older brother Archie had done well at school and had become a vicar just like their dad. James was more of a dreamer. School bored him and he disliked his dad's penny-pinching ways. 'What was the point of having money if you never got to enjoy it?' he thought.

Lauchlin had hoped to see his younger son go into business but the vicar died when James was eighteen (and still struggling with his schoolwork). Lauchlin's fortune was divided between his two sons. What had taken Lauchlin years to save, James blew in months. He bought silk waistcoats and expensive leather shoes. He held groovy parties, where guests drank only the best champagne. He took up gambling and gave lavish gifts to girls who wore far too much make-up. When the money was all gone James had to take a job as a butler. A servant's pay was not enough for James. He started stealing from his boss and was caught and sacked. He sold the last of his remaining possessions and moved to London.

Here he met Plunkett. Not a great deal is known about him. We don't even know what his first name was (unless, of course, it was Plunkett and it's his last name that's been lost!) He had been an apothecary, a kind of chemist. After teaming up with James he threw away his test tubes and became a fun-loving criminal!

The devious duo devised a fiendish scam. James would pretend to be a rich Irish lord and Plunkett would pose as his faithful butler. They hoped to con some wealthy widow into marrying James and then make off with all her money.

On paper it looked foolproof. What woman could resist such a charming, handsome Irish gentleman? The pair wined and dined dozens of women. James sent love notes. He showered them with gifts and compliments. He begged rich woman after rich woman to be his bride. The women were all tremendously flattered. The gifts and notes were lovely. The food and the wine were delicious. It was just so nice to be taken out for dinner once in a while. But marry this slip of a boy? Not on your nelly. There was something fishy about him and his odd little butler. (Cough mixture instead of afternoon tea? It just wasn't the done thing.)

Having squandered all their money wining and dining rich women, James and Plunkett found they were flat broke. In desperation they decided to hold up a coach. They rode out to Hounslow Heath and hid in a small clump of trees by the roadside. After half an hour a carriage trundled by.

James was very nervous. He could barely hold his pistol he was shaking so much.

'Stand and deliver! Your money or your wife!' James bellowed.'

'But I am not married,' said a man's voice from inside the coach.

'Not married? What on earth do you mean?' asked James (oblivious to his silly mistake. He had meant to say life, not wife!).

'Well, I am not married so I can't offer you my wife instead of money. I was engaged once. Estella was her name. Lovely girl from Smithfield. Broke my heart.'

James was getting confused. Who on earth was Estella? What was this man going on about? 'Will you just shut up and give me your money!' he yelled.

'You did ask. I was only trying to answer your question. I don't know, young people are so rude these days.'

'OK, OK, I'm sorry. I'm new to this. Will you please, please just give me all your money?'

'I'm not sure. You offered me a choice. It's not fair if I haven't got a wife.'

'Er ... I don't understand,' said James.

'Look, just suppose I had married Estella,' the man continued.

'Yes,' said James cautiously.

'Well, by now we would have been married for thirty years. It could be time for a change. We might have got bored with each other. You know, stuck in a rut. Estella might fancy a new, wild life on the road. And I could return to being a carefree bachelor once again.'

'Um ... I see your point,' said James. This really was a tricky one. He thought about it for a moment. Plunkett, who had been quietly listening until then, came up with a very simple solution.

He strode toward the coach and pointed the barrels of both his pistols through the open window.

'I am going to count to three. If by the time I get to three you have not handed over all your cash, I will blow your head off.'

Without another word a purse with 60 guineas (gold coins) in it came flying out of the coach.

After that James and Plunkett never looked back. They

stole so much money that James rented two flats. One was in St James's, the hippest part of town. The other was in then up-and-coming Chelsea. Plunkett had a plush house in Jermyn Street, Piccadilly.

James could now afford to pass himself off as an Irish lord and he did. He mingled with London's wealthiest people. He went to the fanciest shops and restaurants. He spent a small fortune on clothes. He wore bright red silk coats with lace trimmings; pairs of black velvet breeches (knee-length trousers); white silk stockings and pairs of yellow Morocco slippers. At night, though, he put on a simple black cloak and a mask and toured the highways with Plunkett.

One evening in 1749 they found themselves robbing the prime minister's son, Horace Walpole!

Horace had spent the evening at Holland House in Kensington. It's now a posh part of town but then Kensington was a village on the edge of the city.

Horace was taking a risk. He had to cross Hyde Park to get back into London. Hyde Park was a very dangerous place after dark. People going out of town at night would meet at the watchman's hut at Hyde Park Corner. For safety, they would then travel across the park in groups armed with swords, clubs and blunderbusses (shot guns).

# Highwayman Hotspot

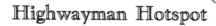

In 1736 Lord Hervey, a fop who lived in Kensington, wrote that:

*The Road between this place and London is grown so infamously bad that we live here in the same solitude as we should do as if cast on a rock in the middle of the ocean; and all Londoners tell us there is between them and us a great impassable gulf.*

In other words no one went to or from Kensington unless they really had to!

Around the same time a highwayman robbed King George II of his watch at Kensington Palace! The king was sitting in his own garden. The highwayman rode up to the hedge, peered over and politely asked the king to hand over his valuables!

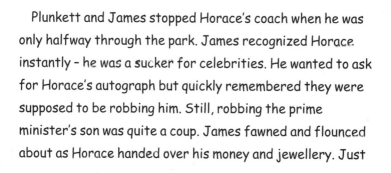

Plunkett and James stopped Horace's coach when he was only halfway through the park. James recognized Horace instantly – he was a sucker for celebrities. He wanted to ask for Horace's autograph but quickly remembered they were supposed to be robbing him. Still, robbing the prime minister's son was quite a coup. James fawned and flounced about as Horace handed over his money and jewellery. Just before James was about to mount his horse he gave Horace a little bow. As he bent down his gun went off accidentally. A bullet whistled by Horace's face, grazing his cheek. Shocked James and Plunkett galloped off into the night.

James was so embarrassed that the next day he sent Horace a letter of apology. Worried that he hadn't grovelled enough, he sent another one and got Plunkett to write one too!

## Highwayman Hotspot

### As Safe as the Houses of Parliament

In your school they may ring a bell to mark the end of the day. In the Houses of Parliament, the police in the chamber shout, 'Who goes home?' ('We do,' think the MPs gleefully!) This chant goes back to the time when the London streets were so scary that MPs didn't dare leave alone! Footpads and highwaymen would rob right outside the Houses of Parliament! So that they weren't robbed (or murdered) politicians were led to their coaches by armed guards. To hurry the politicians along – MPs were chatterboxes even in the old days – the guards would bellow 'Who goes home?'

They decided to lie low for a bit. However, as they were both such big spenders it wasn't long before they were back on the road!

James's love of fashion proved to be their undoing. On the evening of 26 June 1750 they carried out two robberies. At Turnham Green they held up a coach and made off with watches, jewels and money. One of the passengers was wearing a very expensive embroidered waistcoat. James just couldn't resist it and so stole it as well. Later in the evening they held up another coach on Hounslow Heath and this time James nicked a rakish red coat.

The next day James tried to sell the clothes. Unfortunately a reward had been offered for their return and James was arrested. He said his friend Plunkett had asked him to sell them. He claimed to be an Irish lord who knew nothing about highway robbery. Meanwhile, Plunkett had vanished. (He was never seen nor heard of again.) Many of James's posh mates swore he was a good egg. It was no good. He was sentenced to death on 13 September 1750. In the weeks before his execution over 3,000 people visited him in his Newgate Prison cell. Now *he* was a celebrity! Books, poems, songs and plays were written about him. Ever the dandy, James went to Tyburn on 3 October 1750 dressed in his best silk waistcoat and wearing his favourite pair of yellow slippers. (What a fashion victim!)

# Buttonboy Billy

Billy Page grew up in the country in the 1730s. His folks were farmers. Little Billy was scared of the cows and the sheep. They smelled of poo and the straw they slept on itched his skin. His parents realized that he'd never make a good farmer, so when he was ten they sent him to London to live with his cousin. Billy's cousin ran a shop that sold threads, ribbons and buttons. Billy was taught how to sew and was put to work in the shop. Billy enjoyed his new life. He liked playing around with the ribbons and buttons. He kept an eye on all the latest trends and customers would always ask his advice on what to buy. Were big buttons in this spring? Did this or that thread match the dress? Was yellow ribbon only for tying around oak trees? Buttonboy Billy knew. He soon became so obsessed with fashion that he would sometimes stay up all night altering his own clothes by candlelight! At first, his cousin was happy for Billy to use ribbons and buttons from the shop. If the buttons looked good on Billy, customers would probably want to buy them too. However, Billy was using so much of the best stuff, his cousin decided to dock his wages. Billy responded by pinching money from the till. He was caught and flung out on his ear.

Billy had no money, no home; only the trendy clothes he

was wearing. He managed to borrow a pair of pistols and a horse from a friend. He rode to Blackheath, held up a coach and made off with £4 (not bad for a beginner). The next night his haul was £30. The following day he went straight out and bought a horse and his own pistols. He took a gorgeous flat in Grosvenor Square, Mayfair, and ordered a magnificent new suit. That evening he was back on the road. Within a few weeks he had the best wardrobe in town and a string of girls chasing after him.

In those days there weren't many proper maps of London and no such thing as an A-Z. Billy decided to draw his own maps of all the roads in and out of town. If he got into a jam or needed to make a hasty getaway he would know every shortcut in the city!

As his life of crime continued he began to worry about being caught. He decided to adopt a new disguise. Instead of riding out on his horse, he would leave his flash pad in a small horse-drawn carriage. That way he would look like he was going out on the town for the evening. Once he was safely out of town he would hide the carriage. He would then change his clothes, put on a mask and cloak, jump on the horse and start to rob coaches. When he'd finished he'd change back into his dandy clothes, take off the mask and cloak, chain the horse to the coach and ride back to Mayfair as if he'd spent the evening at the theatre. None of the neighbours suspected that the rich, young fop was actually a highwayman.

## Highwayman Hotspot

Buttonboy Billy wasn't Mayfair's only highwayman. In 1768 one highwayman used what was then Lansdowne Passage – it is now part of Lansdowne Row – in Mayfair to make his escape after robbing a coach at Piccadilly. To stop this happening again a whopping great iron bar was put up across the street. The iron bar stood there until the beginning of the 1900s.

However, one night things went a bit wrong. Billy had robbed some travellers near Putney. After he finished stuffing his pockets with loot he rode off to collect his carriage and head for home. When he got there however there was one problem. The carriage and his set of smart clothes had been nicked. The robber had been robbed! He spotted wheel marks in the mud and decided to follow them and nab the crooks.

After about ten minutes he caught up with his carriage. It was being pulled over Putney Common by a group of haymakers. He was just about to ride after them and demand at gunpoint its return, when who should appear? The very travellers he had robbed earlier on! The travellers, seeing the posh carriage, were convinced that the haymakers were part of the highwayman's gang. They demanded their money back. This gave Billy an idea.

He jumped off his horse and stripped to his underwear. He smeared his face with mud and limped toward the haymakers and travellers. He accused the haymakers of beating him up and then stealing his clothes and carriage. The haymakers denied it. The travellers, who didn't recognize Billy, believed his story. The Law was summoned. Billy was easily able to prove the carriage was his and the haymakers found themselves in gaol! With the carriage and his clothes back Billy, wisely, dropped the charges and they were allowed to go free.

Billy returned to horseback. He kept the carriage but from then onwards he only used it when he really was going to theatre!

For the next three years Billy teamed up with another highwayman called Darwell. The pair carried out over 300 daring robberies but in the end Darwell caused Billy's downfall. In April of 1758 Billy and Darwell were caught holding up a coach. Billy managed to escape. Darwell didn't. Darwell was offered the chance of a pardon if he helped the authorities catch Billy. He didn't want to betray his friend but the choice was stark. If he helped he could walk free. If he didn't he would be hanged.

Darwell told them where he was hiding – the Golden Lion tavern near Hyde Park – and Billy was quickly arrested. Darwell was pardoned. Billy was hanged.

## Sixteen String Jack

Sixteen String Jack was nimble. Sixteen String Jack was quick. Sixteen String Jack had sixteen strings. They were actually brightly coloured silk ribbons tied round his knees. Sixteen String Jack was really called John. Before he was a highwayman, humble old John Rann had been a coachman. He worked for a rich gentleman who lived in Portman Square, London. He soon grew to envy his boss's luxurious lifestyle. All the man and his chums did was swagger around town in their best clothes. He treated John little better than his least favourite dog – a spaniel called Russell. Just as he bellowed and kicked Russell when the beast refused to come to heel, he ordered John about, clipped him around the head, called him a fool and constantly criticized his driving. John decided enough was enough. He jacked his job in and became a pickpocket. When he'd stolen enough cash he bought a horse, two pistols, and a mask and became 'Jack' the highwayman.

Jack was short – he was only about five feet five tall – and so was his career as a highwayman. Jack was on the road for less than two years. In that time this little man managed to make a big impression. Jack may have been small but he was good-looking and dressed with style. When he robbed he wore sixteen coloured ribbons tied to his knees. Jack was superstitious and believed they brought him good luck. The ribbons seemed to work. Jack was caught and arrested six times and yet each time he managed to get off scot-free!

After the sixth arrest Jack held a great party in Vauxhall for his friends to celebrate. Jack wore a bright red velvet coat, white silk stockings and a very silly lace hat. At the end of the evening Jack – who was a bit squiffy – hired a carriage and drove through the city streets boldly telling passers-by that he was London's greatest highwayman!

Jack wasn't so lucky the next time. He was caught after robbing a vicar of his watch and a measly 18 pence on the highway near Ealing. Jack was taken to Newgate Prison. Jack was so convinced that he would get off he booked another party for his friends.

However, this time he was found guilty and sentenced to death. On 30 November 1774 Jack was taken to Tyburn. He wore a beautiful pea green suit and, just for luck, he had carefully tied sixteen ribbons to his knees. Unfortunately, there was no escaping the noose and Sixteen String Jack was strung up.

Following his death several books about his wild adventures appeared. He became so famous that even Dr Samuel Johnson praised him. Johnson was the inventor of the dictionary and one of the leading writers in the London of George III (the mad king). He was a hard man to impress. He was grumpy and no oil painting either! One of his eyes was wonky, he didn't wash and his wigs, which didn't fit him, were always singed on one side where he read by candlelight.

In writing about the poet John Gray, Johnson said that Gray's poems 'towered above the ordinary run of verse as Sixteen String Jack above the ordinary footpad'.

# Highwayman Hotspot

The biggest box office smash of the 1700s was a play all about a brave young highwayman – *The Beggar's Opera* by John Gay. The play was first performed in 1728 at the Lincoln's Inn theatre. It was so successful that Gay's business partner John Rich used the money he made to build the Covent Garden Opera House. There is still an opera house on the same site today!

Not everyone liked the play. Like some television cop shows or gangster films now, many people thought that the play encouraged people to commit crime.

Grumpy Samuel Johnson (see p.60) was worried about it but he doubted 'that any man was ever made a rogue' by seeing it.

Another writer, the historian Edward Gibbon, thought the play might be a good thing. He believed that highwaymen who saw it would become 'less ferocious, more polite and in short more like gentlemen'.

# CHAPTER SIX

# Wicked Women

So far we've only discussed highwaymen but there was no shortage of women who donned masks and took to the roads. Most chose to disguise themselves as men but a few used some good old fashioned 'girl power' to get what they wanted.

## No Doll Moll

Moll Cutpurse was a fence. She wasn't made of wood or wire and she didn't stand in a garden. Crooks in the old days used a kind of slang called 'cant' when they talked to each other – like cockney rhyming slang. A 'fence' was someone who sold stolen goods. If you were a highwayman or pickpocket it was safer not to sell stolen loot yourself. You took your loot to a fence. If the fence thought they could sell the goods they would buy them from you at a knock-down price. They would then sell them on for a profit. So, Moll really was a fence! Before she became a fence she had been a thief and was for a while a highwaywoman. Moll's real name was Mary Frith. Moll is short for Mary and 'Cutpurse' was cant for thief – in other words someone who 'cut' purses away from their owners.

Moll was born in about 1589. At that time Queen Elizabeth I, another feisty woman, was on the throne. Moll was the daughter of a shoemaker. Her family lived in the Barbican in the City of London. Little Moll was a tomboy. She didn't want to play with dolls or wear pretty dresses. She loved fighting, climbing trees and swimming in the Thames. When she grew up she dressed like a man. Women in those days were supposed to wear long uncomfortable skirts. Moll wore trousers. Women then were supposed to speak quietly and never to disagree with anything a man said. Moll didn't give two figs what other people thought. If she believed anyone – man or woman – was talking rubbish she told them so.

Walter Raleigh (Queen Elizabeth's favourite explorer, you know, he was the one who put his coat over a puddle) had just brought tobacco into England. (He also brought potatoes to Britain too. Imagine life without chips or crisps!) Smoking was the latest craze. It was also deadly but back then they had no idea it caused cancer. If you were a young man it was trendy to smoke a pipe. Cigarettes hadn't yet been invented. You might smell horrible but they stupidly thought it looked cool. Women weren't supposed to smoke but Moll, surprise, surprise, had a great big pipe and smoked like a chimney.

Moll was the queen of London's criminal underworld. She knew every crook in town. Thieves flocked to her house on Fleet Street. Moll became so rich and so famous that in 1611 a play called *The Roaring Girl* was written all about her crooked life. Moll didn't die until 1663 so they missed some of her greatest crimes!

As a highwaywoman Moll held up one of Oliver Cromwell's top generals on Hounslow Heath. General Thomas Fairfax was a tough military man from Yorkshire. He was a Puritan and in the English Civil War he fought against King Charles I. He was scared of no one. When Moll stopped his carriage he refused to hand over his money. Moll was used to getting her own way. She shot him in the arm. (It was armed robbery!) She then grabbed his bag, which was full of 250 gold coins, and rode off at full speed. Moll forced her horse to ride so fast that the nag was exhausted by the time they reached Turnham Green. The horse sat down and refused to go any further. Moll swore and kicked the horse but it was no good. The horse wouldn't budge. While the horse sat nibbling the grass and getting his breath back Moll was arrested! She was taken off to Newgate Gaol. But Moll didn't stay in prison long. She bribed the judge, giving him £2000 (a fortune then). This queen of crime somehow always managed to cheat the gallows. Moll eventually died in her sleep at the ripe old age of seventy-four.

# Kate Ferrers: The Flame-Haired Thief

Kate Ferrers was another highwaywoman who dressed as a man. Unlike Moll, Kate only wore boys' clothes when she was robbing. Kate was extremely beautiful with long flame-coloured hair and sparkling green eyes. She was a rich aristocrat. She didn't need to steal for money. She did it for fun!

When Kate was eighteen her mean old dad forced her to marry a lord who had stacks of cash. Kate's husband was kind but he was twice her age and very ugly. Lord Ferrers had a huge country mansion in Hemel Hempstead, Hertfordshire, and a big house in Lincoln's Inn, Holborn. The lord often left his new wife all alone in Hemel Hempstead while he enjoyed himself in London. Kate was bored out of her mind in the country. She wanted some fun. She wanted to go dancing. She wanted to chat to interesting people. She wanted to be as far away from Hemel Hempstead as possible.

Kate got so fed up that she decided to become a highwaywoman. One night she borrowed some of her husband's clothes and took to the roads near her home. She was nervous but buzzing with excitement. She spotted a coach heading in the direction of her house. Kate rode up to it. Putting on her deepest voice she shouted: 'Stand and deliver! Your money or your life!' There was no turning back now. A woman inside the carriage cried out in horror. Kate recognized the voice. It was her husband's interfering sister, Lizzie, Kate's own sister-in-law! Kate detested Lizzie. She was always telling Kate what to do and moaning about the weather. This was going to be fun, she thought. Lizzie looked straight at Kate as she handed over her jewels but still didn't recognize her! What a silly fool Lizzie was, Kate thought.

When the robbery was over, Kate galloped home and quickly changed back into her dress. With only moments to spare Lizzie's coach turned up at the house. Lizzie, helped by the coach driver, staggered into Kate's sitting room.

'Oh Kate, something terrible has happened. I've just been robbed on my way here by a terrible highwayman!'

'How dreadful!' Kate replied. Trying hard not to giggle she added, 'Sit down, let me get you some brandy and you must tell me all about it.'

Kate fetched a glass of brandy and helped Lizzie into a chair.

When Lizzie was settled, Kate began to quiz her. She asked her where the robbery had happened and what the crook had taken. When she began to ask about the highwayman himself she got some interesting answers ...

'What did he look like?' Kate asked.

'Oh ... he was very tall with thick dark curly hair,' Lizzie answered.

Kate smirked. She was only five feet tall.

'Was he handsome?' Kate wondered.

'Oh, yes, very. He had a big, booming deep voice. He was so charming. He said, "Madame I will rob you of your jewels but please never rob the world of your beauty."'

Kate nearly choked. She spluttered, 'Oh, how brave you were! I feel quite faint. The idea of such a fiend is making me light-headed. To think you stood up to a big, tall highwayman all by yourself! I would have just screamed and given him all my jewels.'

'Well, Kate, I am just made of sterner stuff than you. If only you took my advice sometimes ...'

Kate could barely keep a straight face. She wanted to laugh so much her stomach hurt. After Lizzie had gone she changed back into her husband's clothes and went straight back out on her horse. That night she held up three more coaches!

In the summer of 1683 Kate terrorized travellers on Watling Street, the old Roman road that ran from London to St Albans in Hertfordshire. One night she came face to face with a handsome young highwayman called Jerry Jackson. They became good friends and would sometimes rob together.

No one knows what eventually happened to Kate. Her robberies stopped after 1684. Many people believe she was caught and hanged. Others think that she simply returned to being a bored housewife. Some say that she ran away with Jerry Jackson. Her life story inspired a novel,

*The Wicked Lady*, and two films!

---

## Highwayman Hotspot

In the 1720s the road between Shoreditch and Cheshunt really was a highwayman hotspot! It became so dangerous that in 1722 the men who worked at the Shoreditch turnpike – the road's turnstile or gateway – were given trumpets. These weren't to play tunes on but to sound the alarm if highwaymen were afoot. The trumpets turned out to be a great success. A local newspaper reported that for two months there were no highway robberies there at all. (Talk about blowing your own trumpet!)

---

# The Cornhill Coach Robber

Nan Hereford didn't dress up as a man. Nan was a wily highwaywoman. She didn't fancy all that cloak wearing and 'money or your life' stuff so she cooked up a scam. Nan would put on her best frock and the kind of mask people wore to balls. She then got six friends to dress up as adoring footmen and would drive around Westminster, Cheapside and Cornhill in a dainty little coach pretending she was a princess. Rich men catching sight of this grand young lady would ride alongside her carriage, doff their hats and ask her for a date. Nan would pretend to be flattered and then fast as you like whip out a dinky pistol and rob them on the spot.

This scam worked well for several months but one day Nan tried to lure a wealthy merchant into her trap. The merchant grew suspicious and followed her carriage. He caught her trying to rob a linen draper's coach on Cornhill. Nan was bundled off to Newgate Prison. In prison she tried to escape by setting fire to the gaol! She was discovered and clapped in heavy iron chains. As a warning to other prisoners who might try the same thing, Nan was hanged right in front of the gaol on 22 December 1690.

## The Cheapside Cheat

Mary Ann Meders was known as the German Princess. She wasn't German and she wasn't a princess. Mary Ann was born in Canterbury in Kent in 1642, her dad was the choirmaster at Canterbury Cathedral. Young Mary Ann was no singing angel. She was a rebel and a cheat. At fifteen she ran away from home and married a shoemaker from Maidstone called

Stedman. She quickly got bored of Stedman. She left him and moved to Dover. Here she met a nice young doctor who asked Mary Ann to marry him. Mary Ann, who hadn't bothered to tell him she already had a husband, gleefully accepted. Shortly after the ceremony news of her previous marriage leaked out and Mary Ann fled to London. In the capital she wasted no time in getting herself another husband. (Third time lucky!)

Hubby number three, John Carleton, was a wealthy man and Mary Ann happily spent as much of his money as she could. She bought herself jewels, the finest silk dresses and the most elegant shoes. Somehow John's brother Charles got to hear about her other marriages. He went to see Mary Ann and threatened to tell John. Mary Ann claimed both her previous husbands were dead. Charles was not convinced. Mary Ann decided not to risk exposure. She packed as many of her jewels as she could carry and took a ship to Holland. She then travelled to Cologne in Germany. While in Germany Mary Ann pretended to be a rich English countess. She booked into expensive lodgings but always sneaked away without paying her bills.

After about six months she was running out of money (and lodging houses to rip off!) so in March 1663 she returned to London. She took rooms in The Exchange Tavern in Billingsgate. Mary Ann adopted a fake German accent and claimed to be the daughter of a German prince, Lord Henry von Wolway. She fooled everyone. She had a string of wealthy admirers, including an elderly lord who showered her with gifts and begged her to be his mistress. She strung him along and borrowed enough money from him to move to plusher rooms in Cheapside. One evening the old fool called on her and let slip that he had £200 in gold in his coach. No sooner had he left than Mary Ann called for her own carriage. She chased after him and held him up at pistol point! Mary Ann was so impressed with her skill as a highway robber that she later held up three of her other admirers as well!

Mary Ann's other scam was to defraud the French silk weavers who lived around Spitalfields. She would order reams of elegantly embroidered silk, only paying a small deposit to start with. When the cloth was finished she'd ask the weaver to bring it to her lodgings. The weaver would arrive and Mary Ann would give him a glass of wine and inspect the cloth. She would praise his work to the skies. 'Oh, what a clever weaver you are, monsieur!' she would say. Putting on her thickest fake German accent she would add, 'These English have no understanding of beauty! You, sir, are an artist!' She went on like this for about half an hour until the weaver had a head the size of Luxembourg.

Mary Ann would then announce that she simply must show

the silk to her little niece, Charlotte. Of course, Mary Ann didn't have a niece called Charlotte! She'd tell the weaver that her 'niece' was a sickly child. Charlotte, poor dear, was lying in a bed in the very next room! (Surely the little girl was bound to perk up if she saw such wonderful silk!) Mary Ann would nip next door, taking the silk with her. The weaver was left to sit and wait. He'd sip his wine and twiddle his thumbs. After about twenty minutes he'd start to feel uneasy. He'd knocked on the door but there was no answer. He soon found that Mary Ann and his precious silk had vanished! Later, he'd discover that the room had only been hired for the day and that no one had any idea who Mary Ann was or where she had gone. Mary Ann pulled this stunt several times all over London.

She may have been a great conwoman and a nifty highwaywoman but she was a lousy thief. Her life of crime came to an end when she was caught stealing a silver plate from a house on Chancery Lane. At her trial she still maintained she was a real German princess. It made no difference. She was sentenced to death and hanged at Tyburn on 2 January 1673.

# CHAPTER SEVEN

# The Truth about Turpin

The most famous highwayman of all time is Dick Turpin. His daring robberies are the stuff of London legend. His ghost is thought to haunt the Spaniard's Inn in Hampstead and has been spied eerily galloping across Hampstead Heath. His exploits have long been celebrated in books, films and songs (ask your mum or dad about 1980s popstar Adam Ant!).

Usually Dick is portrayed as a dashing romantic hero but the real Turpin was a nasty piece of work. Dick was an ugly, violent thug. He was short, hairy and his face was scarred by smallpox, a hideous disease that causes the skin to break out in pus-filled pimples.

The real Dick Turpin was born in an Essex pub in 1705. Young Dick learned to read and write, still unusual in those days, and when he was about sixteen he trained as a butcher in Whitechapel. Dick set up his own butcher's shop back in Essex a couple of years later but he got into debt. He started to steal cattle in Plaistow. It wasn't long before Dick had branched out into burglary. He joined the Gregory Gang, a vicious gang of Essex housebreakers. The gang terrorized London during the summer of 1735 until Gregory, the gang's leader, was caught and hanged.

The gang split up and Dick became a highwayman.

Dick quickly made his name as a highwayman. His raids on coaches on the highroads of Essex and on Barnes and Finchley Commons and Hampstead Heath were reported in the *Grub Street Journal* and *London Gazette* newspapers.

## Highwayman Hotspot

### Turpin's Town

Dick may have been born in Hempstead, Essex, but he loved old London town! There are hundreds of Turpin top spots across the city – there's even a street named after him – Turpin's Way in Holloway. Here are just a few.

### Hampstead

A ghostly figure thought to be Dick has been seen galloping over Hampstead Heath – one of his favourite haunts while he was alive. The spooky sound of horses' hooves has also been heard echoing around the old stables of The Spaniard's Inn in Hampstead.

## Finchley Common

Another favourite haunt of Dick's. An old oak tree used to stand in the centre of the common. It was called Turpin's Oak in his honour.

## Hackney Marsh

Today it's a sports field but Dick used to rob here.

## Broadway SW1

This street near St James's Park is now the home of New Scotland Yard Police station but super crook Dick Turpin once lived here!

## Saffron Hill and Hatton Gardens, Clerkenwell

In Turpin's time this whole area was a den of thieves. Dick came here to sell his stolen goods to 'fences' – people like Moll Cutpurse. It was a still a hot bed of crooks a century after Dick's death. The great London writer Charles Dickens set *Oliver Twist*, his classic novel about pickpockets, here.

## Westminster

The Black Horse Inn on Westminster Broadway always maintained that Dick began his famous, but completely fictional, ride to York after drinking a pint of beer here.

**Peckham Rye**

A road made of white stones once ran across the Rye. This was called Dick's Ride because the highwayman was thought to have used it to flee the city.

**Regent's Park**

In Dick's day the park was called Marylebone Gardens. It was then a popular weekend amusement park with a bowling green. Dick came here to stroll, gamble and (of course) rob.

During one robbery Dick found himself face to face with another highwayman, Robert King. Robert was delighted. (Highway robbery can be lonely work!) 'What! Dog eat dog,' he exclaimed. 'Come, come, brother Turpin, if you don't know me I know you, and should be glad of your company!'

They became partners in crime. The pair would rob on the roads outside London and then return to a secret hideout in the heart of Epping Forest.

## Highwayman Hotspot

Dick Turpin and Robert King weren't the first outlaws to hide in Epping Forest.

During the 1690s England was at war with France. In this period England's army became enormous. However, in 1698 a peace deal was signed at the Treaty of Ryswick. The war was over but this left tons of soldiers without jobs. Unable to make an honest living some became highwaymen. One group of thirty former soldiers lived as bandits in Epping Forest. They built huts near Waltham Cross and at night they crept out to prey on travellers journeying to and from London.

Dick and Robert's partnership came to a messy end in May 1737. They were on their way into town when Dick's horse, Dobbin, or whatever he was called, became tired. Dick spotted a man riding a nice sleek horse with white markings on its legs. He held the man up and made off with his money and his horse, leaving poor Dobbin behind! Now, this new horse turned out to be none other than White Stockings, a prize racehorse. As famous horses went, he couldn't really have stolen a more famous one.

Posters of White Stockings were plastered all over London. The horse's odd white legs made him easy to identify. Within a few days he was seen in the stables of the Red Lion Inn, Whitechapel. The authorities were contacted and the pub was raided. During the scuffle to arrest the highwaymen, Dick accidentally shot and fatally wounded Robert! Some gallant highwayman, eh? The real Dick was such a terrible shot that he managed to kill his own partner! Who needs enemies with friends like that!

Dick escaped but by now a £200 reward – a huge amount then – was offered for his arrest. Dick moved to Welton in Yorkshire after lying low in Lincoln for a few weeks first. When he did finally reach Yorkshire he lived under a false name, John Palmer, and pretended to be an honest horse dealer.

# Honest John's Horse Emporium
## (Est London 1737)

 *Four legs for less!*

## London transport at Yorkshire prices!

*Honest, luv, she's only done 200 miles on the clock!
Her last owner was a little old lady who only rode
her to church on Sundays. A very economical
runner this one, does 40 miles to a bag of hay. Look
at these horseshoes! They're quality. The very latest
design. Scuff resistant and aerodynamically
shaped, they come with a lifetime guarantee.
(The lifetime of a house fly, of course.) You don't
often see craftsmanship like that this far north.
King George II himself has had them fitted on all
his horses. (Or was it houses? I don't speak German
and his English isn't great . . . so who can say?)
Tell you what, I'm robbing myself really (that really
would make a change) but take this horse and I'll
throw in a spare set of shoes. Swear on me old ma's*

One evening, he shot a chicken during a drunken argument with his landlord and wound up in gaol. The Yorkshire authorities had no idea that they had arrested Dick Turpin.

In prison Dick wrote to his brother in Essex to ask for help. By chance the letter found its way to Mr Smith, the local village schoolteacher – the man who had taught Dick to read and write. Smith recognized Dick's handwriting and travelled to Yorkshire. He confirmed that the man they were holding was not John Palmer – dodgy horse salesman and chicken killer – but Dick Turpin, England's most wanted highwayman! Dick was executed at York on Saturday 7 April 1739.

Dick may have been executed but his legend continued to grow. Nearly a hundred years later a writer called William Harrison Ainsworth (who lived in Kilburn) wrote a thrilling novel all about Dick called *Rookwood*. Published in 1834 it went on to become a huge bestseller. It was the *Harry Potter* of its day! In the novel Ainsworth turned dastardly Dick into a dashing hero and gave him a beautiful horse called Black Bess. In one chapter Dick escapes capture by galloping from London to York in a single day. There were no motorways or highspeed trains back then so this was quite a feat. Brave Black Bess is so exhausted after the ride she collapses and dies! Dick, the ungrateful crook, leaves Bess dead by the road. He then wanders off and plays a game of bowls! (I think Ainsworth lost the plot there!)

The story of the ride to York was so gripping and exciting that most readers believed it was true. Today Ainsworth's book is largely forgotten but many people still believe that Dick rode to York and Black Bess is part of the whole Turpin legend.

# THE HOXTON SAUSAGE

*Straight from the horse's mouth!*

**1d**

This week, only in your sensational sizzling *Sausage*,
Dick Turpin's horse Black Bess reveals what life with
London's most notorious highwayman was really like!

# Black Beauty and the Beast

## SHE TALKS ABOUT...

The wild nights on the road

The temper tantrums and the fights

The drinking and the gambling

The women and...

What really happened on that infamous ride to York...

# CHAPTER EIGHT

# The End of the Road

## Jerry the Juvenile Delinquent

As the 1700s came to an end so did the reign of the highwayman. The last London highwayman to become a celebrity was Louis Jeremiah Abershaw. He was known as Jerry to his friends, enemies and victims, which was about everyone really. Jerry was a teenage terror. He was only seventeen when he became a highwayman and he was executed at the grand old age of twenty-two.

Jerry was born in Kingston, Surrey, in 1773 and as a highwayman his favourite patch was always South London. He was the leader of a nasty gang who terrorized the roads between Putney and Wimbledon. His career ended after he was arrested for killing a member of the Bow Street Runners (London's first police force, more about them next) in a tavern in Southwark.

At his trial in Croydon he showed no remorse for the murder. He even laughed and put his hat on when the judge sentenced him to death. While he was waiting to be executed Jerry spent his time daubing the walls of his prison cell with graffiti. On the morning of Monday 3 August 1795 he was taken to Kennington Common to be hanged.

While being driven along in the cart he blew kisses to the crowds. As he approached the gallows he put a flower in his mouth. Jerry's mum had once told him that if didn't stop stealing he would die with his boots on (i.e. not in his bed). When he climbed onto the scaffold Jerry kicked his boots off just to prove her wrong!

Like Frank Jackson, Jerry's dead body was bound in chains and strung up on a gibbet on Wimbledon Hill as a warning to others.

# Here Come the Coppers

One of the reasons London was so popular with highwaymen, footpads and pickpockets was that there was no police force for the capital until the end of the 1700s!

Local people had to police themselves, a bit like Neighbourhood Watch schemes today. A team of nosy parkers from each borough or street had to patrol the city each evening. Not many people wanted to do this. At night, London was dark, dingy, dangerous and there were lots of criminals about. (No change from the daytime then!) The job usually fell to frail old men who were simply hopeless at catching crooks.

In 1748 the writer Henry Fielding was made a magistrate (a minor judge) at Bow St Law Courts. He was so appalled by the corrupt and clumsy clods that guarded the city that he sacked them. He found six men he trusted and gave them jobs as constables. These Bow St Runners, as they were called, became London's first proper police force.

In their first month Henry's Runners succeeded in capturing a notorious gang of highwaymen. Henry wrote to the government and begged for more money to increase the number of patrols. Henry asked for £600. Reluctantly the penny-pinching politicians gave him £200. After the first year Henry's men were arresting as many as forty highwaymen a week!

By this time Henry's blind half-brother John had joined the team. John, who was nicknamed 'The Blind Beak', claimed to be able to recognize over 300 crooks by the sound of their voices alone. When Henry died in 1754 John took over at Bow Street. John set up night patrols on the turnpikes – the gates – into the city. The numbers of highway robberies fell dramatically but the government still refused to give him any more funds. John had to account for every single penny he spent even to get what little money they did offer.

ໃຈ

# Bow Street Runners
## The Old Bill

| | |
|---|---|
| Waylaying a highwayman at a Turnpike | 5 shillings |
| Pursuing a highwayman near Hackney | 17 shillings and 6 pence |
| Guarding a wounded highwayman in hospital | £1 and 11 shillings and 6 pence |
| Pursuing and apprehending Jonathan Wigmore, highwayman, for attempting to rob the King of Poland's Groom | £8 and 8 shillings |
| Total | £11 and 2 shillings |

*(Service not Included)*

ໃຈ

John eventually ran out of cash and had to stop the patrols. The crafty highwaymen, spotting the roads were clear again, returned in droves. By the 1770s things were as bad as before and yet the government still refused to fork out for a police force.

Patrols didn't return until 1805. In 1829 a brand new police force for the whole of London was established by Robert Peel – they were nicknamed Bobbies after their founder.

By then highwaymen were already in sharp decline. The city had changed and highwaymen hadn't kept up. All this Stand and Deliver stuff was old hat!

## The Crimes they were a' Changin

In 1797 the prime minister, William Pitt, had brought in radical new laws to control the nation's then rocky finances. His Bank Restriction Act introduced income tax and replaced many of the gold coins with paper 'banknotes' and cheques. It was soon considered unfashionable to carry great lumps of gold about the place. If you were rich you now paid by cheque, or used a crisp new banknote! This was bad news for highwaymen. The easy-to-steal gold coins were gone. Highwaymen couldn't cash cheques and stolen banks notes could be traced!

By the time Queen Victoria was on the throne London was growing in size. What had once been tiny villages on the outskirts of town, perfect spots for highway robbery, were now parts of the city. New houses were popping up everywhere. There were fewer places for horse-riding bandits to hide!

Then the railways arrived. Steam trains started to replace coaches. Bellowing 'Your money or your life?' at a thundering iron beast was a waste of time. The train driver couldn't hear a word you said. Even if they did, they weren't likely to stop for some fool on a horse wearing a frilly shirt and a mask. The age of London's noble rogues of the road was well and truly over. Not everyone was pleased to see them go, however. Although there was now a police force, London was still plagued by pickpockets, burglars and thieves. Compared to highwaymen, modern crooks looked sneaky.

In 1887 the novelist Robert Louis Stevenson – the man who penned the classics *Treasure Island* and *Dr Jekyll and Mr Hyde* – fondly recalled reading about highwaymen as a boy.

He wrote:

**Give me a highwayman and I was full to the brim ... the highwayman was my favourite dish. I can still hear that merry clatter of hoof along the moonlit lane: night and the coming of day are still related with the doings of Sixteen String Jack or Jerry Abershaw.**

Hope you've enjoyed reading all about them too!

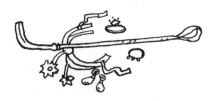

# The Highwayman Quiz

1) How many old pence was a shilling worth in 1800?

2) Which king liked to dress up in green tights and pretend to be Robin Hood?

3) How many people lived in Tudor London?

4) How many people live in London now?

5) What were 'footpads'?

6) Which play by Shakespeare involves highway robbery?

7) What did the highwayman Johnny Popham end up doing?

8) Who was the highwayman's favourite king?

9) What was Mulled Sack named after?

10) Who came to power after Oliver Cromwell died?

11) Why do they say 'Who goes home?' at the end of the day at Parliament?

12) What was a 'fence' in highwayman lingo?

13) Where does the word 'cutpurse' come from?

14) What was the name of Dick Turpin's fabled horse?

15) Why are policemen called Bobbies?

# ANSWERS

1) Twelve
2) Henry VIII
3) 40,000
4) Close on 7 million
5) Robbers who worked on foot
6) Henry IV
7) He became a judge
8) Charles I
9) His favourite tipple - a spicy alcoholic drink
10) Charles I's son, Charles II
11) It's from the days when politicians had to gather in safe numbers when leaving Westminster, because of the many highwaymen waiting to pounce
12) A receiver of stolen goods
13) From 'cutting' purses away from their owners
14) Black Bess - we don't know the name of his real horse
15) After Robert (Bobbie) Peel, the founder of the modern police force

# Other books from Watling St you'll love

## CRYPTS, CAVES AND TUNNELS OF LONDON
By Ian Marchant
Peel away the layers under your feet and discover the
unseen treasures of London beneath the streets.
ISBN 1-904153-04-6

## GRAVE-ROBBERS, CUT-THROATS AND POISONERS OF LONDON
By Helen Smith
Dive into London's criminal past and meet some of its
thieves, murderers and villains.
ISBN 1-904153-00-3

## DUNGEONS, GALLOWS AND SEVERED HEADS OF LONDON
By Travis Elborough
For spine-chilling tortures and blood-curdling punishments,
not to mention the most revolting dungeons and prisons you
can imagine.
ISBN 1-904153-03-8

## THE BLACK DEATH AND OTHER PLAGUES OF LONDON
By Natasha Narayan
Read about some of the most vile and rampant diseases ever
known and how Londoners overcame them – or not!
ISBN 1-904153-01-1

## GHOSTS, GHOULS AND PHANTOMS OF LONDON
By Travis Elborough
Meet some of the victims of London's bloodthirsty
monarchs, murderers, plagues, fires and famines – who've
chosen to stick around!
ISBN 1-904153-02-X

## RATS, BATS, FROGS AND BOGS OF LONDON
By Chris McLaren
Find out where you can find some of the creepiest and crawliest inhabitants of London.
ISBN 1-904153-05-4

## BLOODY KINGS AND KILLER QUEENS OF LONDON
By Natasha Narayan
Read about your favourite royal baddies and their gruesome punishments.
ISBN 1-904153-16-X

## SPIES, SECRET AGENTS AND BANDITS OF LONDON
By Natasha Narayan
Look through the spy hole at some of our greatest spies and their exploits, to how to make your own invisible ink.
ISBN 1-904153-14-3

## PIRATES, SWASHBUCKLERS AND BUCCANEERS OF LONDON
By Helen Smith
Experience the pockmarked and perilous life of an average London pirate and his (or her) adventures.
ISBN 1-904153-17-8

## REBELS, TRAITORS AND TURNCOATS OF LONDON
By Travis Elborough
What could you expect if you were a traitor – and you were discovered? Take your pick from some of the most hideous punishments ever invented.
ISBN 1-904153-15-1

## WITCHES, WIZARDS AND WARLOCKS OF LONDON
By Natasha Narayan
Quite simply the bizarre history of London, full of superstition, magic and plain madness.
ISBN 1-904153-12-7

In case you have difficulty finding any Watling St books in your local bookshop, you can place orders directly through

BOOKPOST
Freepost
PO Box 29
Douglas
Isle of Man
IM99 1BQ

Telephone: 01624 836000

email: bookshop@enterprise.net

D1092693